Frederick Douglass' Speech at Elmira, New York
August 3, 1880

reprinted by
New York History Review
2021

Frederick Douglass' Speech at Elmira, New York - August 3, 1880
by Frederick Douglass. 1880

ISBN: 978-1-950822-14-0

Printed in the United States of America

Cover image:
Frederick Douglass (circa 1880) photograph by Matthew Brady. Albu-
men silver print from glass negative. Gillman Collection. Metropolitan
Museum of Art.

Abraham Lincoln's Emancipation proclamation issued January 1, 1863,
[G. R. Russell] Library of Congress

About his visit to Elmira....

Frederick Douglass was the honored speaker in Elmira, New York on August 3, 1880 at today's Grove Park.

Mr. Douglass' visit was a huge festive event, as African American people in Elmira celebrated the anniversary of Britain's liberation of slaves (1834) and the American Emancipation Proclamation (1863).

Mr. Douglass had a deep connection to Elmira. In 1838, during his escape from slavery, he stayed at the home of Jervis Langdon and his wife in Millport, New York.

Frederick Douglass' speech at Elmira, New York
August 3, 1880 at Hoffman's Grove
(Grove Park)

Mr. President and Friends --
I thank you for this cordial greeting. I hear in it something like the thrilling notes of a welcome home after a long absence. More years of my life and labors have been put into this state than in any other state in the Union.

Anywhere within a hundred miles of the goodly city of Rochester, I feel at home. Within that circumference, for enlightenment, liberality, and civilization, the people have no superiors in this country or any other.

Allow me to thank you, also, for your generous words of sympathy and approval. In respect for this important support to a public man, I have been unusually fortunate.

My 40 years' work in the cause of the oppressed and enslaved has been well observed, well appreciated, and well rewarded. All classes in colors, at home and abroad, have in this way held up my hands. Looking back to these long years of toil and conflict, during which I have had blows to take as well as blows to give, and have sometimes received wounds and bruises, both in body and mind,

my only regret is that I have done so little to lift up and strength-
en my long enslaved and still oppressed people. They make these
remarks to myself because I am standing mainly for a new generation. Most of the men with whom I have lived and labored,
five and 30 years ago, have passed away. There are but few left to
tell the story of the early days of anti-slavery. Scarcely any of the
colored men who advocated the cause during that time are now
on the stage of active life, and I begin to feel lonely. But while I
have the sympathy and approval of men and women like these
before me, I pledge you my last breath on behalf of justice, liberty,
and equality for all men. The day we celebrate is preeminently
the colored man's day. The great event which has distinguished it,
will forever distinguish it from all the other days of the year has
just leave claimed thoughtful attention of statesman and of so-
cial reformers throughout the world. To us, however, West India
Emancipation speaks more to feeling than to thought. It stirred
the heart and filled the soul with grateful sentiments. In the history of our struggle with American slavery, the day we celebrate
has played an important part. Emancipation in the West Indies
was to us the first bright star in a dark and stormy sky, the first
smile after a long providential frown. It conveyed the first ray of
hope to the enslaved of our land by demonstrating the possibility
of Negro freedom. Whoever else may forget or slight its claims,
it will never be other than a memorable and glorious day in the
minds of the colored people of the United States. The story of it

shall be brief and soon told: six and 40 years ago, the first day of this month, the day we are constructively celebrating, there went forth over the blue waters of the Caribbean Sea a great message and hailed with startling shouts of joy and loud and thrilling songs of praise. For on that day, 800,000 people were liberated, set free, and received within the pale of law - civilization and human brotherhood.

How vast was the transformation! In one moment, the tick of a watch, the twinkling of an eye, a glance of the morning sun, saw a bondage of ages ended; saw the slave whip burnt to ashes; saw the slaves' chains melted and powerless, saw the slaves' heavy iron fetters all broken and buried forever. The change was so sudden and so great that in the first moment of it, those who were the subject of hesitated as to what it was. They did not know whether to receive it as a reality or a dream. No wonder they were amazed and doubtful and thought it was too good to be true. But when these long in slaved whipped-scarred bruised and battered victims of the cruel old slave system, were fully assured that the good tidings, which had come across the sea were true, that they were indeed no longer slaves, when they knew that the slave driver's arm had fallen by his side; that the lash was no longer to plow deep furrows into their quivering flesh, and they were no longer to be chained, bought and sold like horses, sheep, and swine, their gratitude knew no bounds; they're feeling manifested itself in the wildest possible forms of expression. They ran about, they danced, they gave it into the blue sky, they leapt into the air, they kneeled, they prayed, they shouted, they rolled up on the ground, they embraced each other, they threw their children high over their heads, and caught them in their arms, they laughed and wept for joy. Those who witnessed the scene say they never saw anything like it before.

But now, I must answer a question or two and thereby defend the custom we are here perpetuating. We are asked why we celebrate West Indian emancipation when we might celebrate American emancipation? Why go abroad, when we might stay at home. The answer is easy. In the first place, human liberty excludes all idea of home and abroad. It is universal and disdains localization. As Lowell says:

When a deed is done for freedom
Through the broad earth's aching breast
Runs a thrill of joy prophetic
Trembling on from East to West

It is bounded by no geographical lines or national limitations. Like the glorious sun in the heavens, its light shines for all. Then this West Indian Emancipation of the forever and glory of liberty standing alone, is worthy of celebration. Rich as this 19th-century is, it is moral and material achievements, and its progress and civilization (and it is very rich). It can claim nothing for itself greater, grander, or more to its credit than this West India

Emancipation.

Whether we can consider the matter of it, or the manner of it, the tree or its fruit is it is alike worthy of thought and memory. Especially is the manner of its accomplishment worthy of consideration. Herein I think it is its best lesson to the world. Here is its most encouraging word to all who toil and trust in the overthrow of injustice, slavery, and oppression in the world.

Great invaluable concessions have been made to the liberties of mankind. They have, however, generally come only at the command of the sword. But this concession was an exception. It came not by the sword, but by the word, not by the brute force of numbers, but by the still small voice of truth; not by barricades, bayonets, and bloody revolution; but by peaceful agitation, not by Divine interference; but the exercises of simple human sentiment.

In this peculiarity, we have its greatest values. It is a revelation of peaceful human power. It shows what can be done against wrong in the world without armies on the earth or angels in the sky. It shows that men have in their own hands the means of putting all their moral and political enemies under their feet and of making this world a good and pleasant dwelling place for mankind if they will but use them. It was a new and much-needed revelation of the power of conscience, and of human brotherhood, overlapping the accident of color and race, a great human event wrought out but human means. For it was the faithful, persistent and enduring enthusiasm of Thomas Clarkson, William Wilberforce, Granville Sharpe, William Knibb, Henry Brougham, Thomas Fowell Buxton, Daniel O'Connell, George Thompson and their noble co-workers that finally thawed the British heart into sympathy for the slave and moved the strong arm of the government in mercy to put an end to his bondage.

Let no American, especially no colored American, with-hold a generous recognition of this glorious achievement. What though is not American, but British; what though it was not Re-publican, but monarchs, what though it was not from the Amer-ican Congress, but from the British Parliament; what though it was not from the chair of the President, but from the throne of a Queen, it was none the less a triumph of right over wrong, of good over evil and a victory for the whole human race. Besides: we may properly celebrate this day because its special relation to our Amer-ican emancipation. In doing this, we do not sacrifice the general to the special, the universal to the local. The cause of human liberty is one the world over. The downfall of slavery under British power met the downfall of slavery, ultimately, under American power, and the downfall of Negro slavery everywhere. But the effect of this great and philanthropic measure, naturally enough, was greater here than elsewhere. Outside the British Empire, no other nation was in a position to feel it so much as we. The stimulus it gave to the American anti-slavery movement was immediately pronounced and powerful. British example became a tremendous lever in the hands of American abolitionists. It did much to shame and discourage the spirit of cast and the advocacy of slavery in church and state. It could not well have been otherwise. No man liveth onto himself.

What is true in this respect of individual men is equally true of nations. Both impart good will to their age in generation. But putting aside this consideration so worthy of thought, we have special reasons for claiming August 1 is the birthday of Negro Emancipation, not only in the West Indies, but in the United States. In spite of our national independence, a common language, a common literature, a common history, and a common civilization make us and keep us still a part of the British nation, if not a part of the British Empire. England can't take no step forward in the pathway of a higher civilization without drawing us in the same direction. She is still the mother country, And the mother, too, of our abolitionist movement. Though her emancipation came in peace and ours in war: though hers cost treasure and ours blood, though hers was the result of a sacred preference, its hours resulted in part from necessity, the motive, and main-spring of the respective measures were the same in both.

The abolitionists of this country have been charged with bringing on the war between the North and South, and in one sense, this is true. Had there been no anti-slavery agitation at the North, there would have been no active anti-slavery anywhere to resist the demands of the slave power at the South, and where there is no resistance, there can be no war.

Resistance to slavery and the extension of slavery invited secession and war to perpetuate and extend the slave system. Thus in the same sense, England is responsible for our Civil War. The abolition of slavery in the West Indies gave life and vigor to the abolitionist movement in America. Clarkson of England gave us in Garrison of America. Granville Sharp of England gave us our Wendell Phillips, and Wilberforce of England gave us our peerless Charles Sumner. These grand men and their brave coworkers here took up the moral thunderbolts which had struck down slavery in the West Indies and held him with increased zeal and power against the gigantic system of slavery here, till goaded to madness, the traffickers in the souls and bodies of men, flew to arms, rent asunder of the Union at the center, and fill the land with hostile armies and 10,000 horrors of war. Out of this tempest, out of this whirlwind and earthquake of war came the abolition of slavery, came in the employment of colored troops, came colored citizens, came colored jurymen, came colored congressman, came colored schools in the South, and came the great amendments of our national Constitution. We celebrate this day too, for the very good reason that we have no other to celebrate. English Emancipation has one advantage over American Emancipation. Hers has a definite anniversary. Ours has none. Like our slaves, the freedom of the Negro has no birthday. No man can tell the day of the month or of the year upon which slavery was abolished in the United States.

We cannot even tell when it began to be abolished. Like the movement of the sea, no man can tell where one wave begins, and another ends. The chains of slavery with us were loosened by degrees. First, we had the struggle in Kansas with the border ruffians. Next, we had John Brown at Harper's Ferry, next the firing upon Fort Sumter, a little while after we had Freemont's order of freeing the slaves of the rebels in Missouri. Then we had General Butler declaring in treating the slaves of rebels as contraband of war, next we had the proposition to arm colored men and make them soldiers for the Union. In 1862, we had a conditional promise of a Proclamation of Emancipation from President Lincoln, and finally, on 1 January 1863, we had the Proclamation itself, and still, the end was not yet. Slavery was bleeding and dying, but it was not dead, and no man can tell just when its foul spirit departed from our land, if indeed it has yet departed, and hence we do not know what day we may probably celebrate as coupled with this great American event. When England behave so badly during our last Civil War, I, for one, felt like giving up these first of August celebrations. But I remember that during that war, there were two Englands, as there were two Americas, and that one was true to liberty, while the other was true to slavery. It was not the England which gave us the West India Emancipation. Not the England of John Bright, and William Edward Forrester that permit at Alabamas to escape from the British ports and pray upon our commerce or that otherwise favorite

slave-holding in the South, but it was England which had done
what it could to prevent West India Emancipation. It was the Tory
party in England, that fought the evolution party at home, and the
same party and was that favorite our slave-holding rebellion. Under
a different name, we had the same or a similar party here, a party
which despised the Negro and consigned him to perpetual slavery;
the party which was willing to allow the American Union to be
slivered into fragments rather than one hair of the head of slavery
should be injured. But Fellow Citizens, I should but very imper-
fectly fulfill the duty of this hour I can't find myself to a merely
historical or philosophical decision discussion of the West Indies
Emancipation.

United States slavery has no existence in our country. The
legal form has been abolished. By the law and the Constitution,
the Negro is a man and a citizen and has all the rights and liberties guaranteed to any other variety of the human family residing in
the United States. He has a country, a flag, and a government and
may legally claim full and complete protection under the laws. It
was the ruling wish, intention, and purpose of the loyal people after
the rebellion was suppressed to have an end to the entire cause of
that calamity by forever putting away the system of slavery and all
its incidents. In pursuance of this idea, the Negro was made free,
made a citizen, made eligible to hold office, to be a juryman, a leg-
islator, and a magistrate. To this end, several amendments to the
Constitution were proposed, recommended they are now a part of

the supreme law of the land, binding alike upon every state and territory of the United States, North and South. Briefly, this is our legal and theoretical condition. This is our condition on paper and parchment. If only from the national statute book, we were left to learn the true condition of the color and race, the result would be altogether creditable to the American people. It would give them a clear title to a place among the most enlightened and liberal nations of the world. We could say of our country, as Curran once said, of England, "the spirit of British Law makes liberty commensurate with and inseparable from the British soil, which proclaims even to the stranger and sojourner the moment he sets his foot upon the British earth, that the ground on which he treads is holy and consecrated by the genius of the universal emancipation." No matter in what language his doom may have been pronounced, no matter what complexion incompatible with freedom, an Indian or an African son may have burnt upon him; no matter in what disastrous battle his liberty may have been cloven down. No matter with what solemnities he may have been devoted on the altar of slavery; the first moment he touches the sacred soil of Britain, the altar and the God sink in together in the dust, his soul walks forth in her own majesty; his body swells beyond the measure of his chains that burst from around him, and he stands redeemed, regenerated, and disenthralled by the irresistible genius of universal emancipation. Now I say that this eloquent tribute to England if only we looked into our own Constitution, might apply to us. In that instrument, we have laid down the law now and forever, that there shall be no slavery or involuntary servitude in this Republic except for crime. We have gone still further: we have led the heavy land of the Constitution upon the matchless meanness of cast as well as the hellblack crime of slavery. We have declared before all the world that there shall be no denial of rights on account of race, color, or previous condition of servitude. The advantage gained in this respect is immense. It is a great thing to have the Supreme Law on the side of justice and liberty. It is the line up to which the nation is destined to march – the law to which the nation's life must ultimately conform. It is a great principle up to which we may educate the people - to this extent, its value exceeds our speech.

But today, in most of the Southern states, the 14th, and 15th amendments, are virtually nullified. The rights which they were intended to guarantee or denied and held in contempt. The citizenship granted in the 14th amendment is practically a mockery, and the right to vote provided for in the 15th amendment is literally stamped out in favor of the government. The old master class is today triumphant, and the newly enfranchised class, in a condition but little above that in which they were found before the rebellion. Do you ask me how, after all, that has been done, the state of things has been made possible? I will tell you. Our reconstruction measures were radically defective. They left the former slave completely in the power of the old master, the loyal citizen in the hands of the disloyal rebel against the government. Wise, grand and comprehensive in scope and design is where the reconstruction measures; high and honorable as were the intentions of the stateside then by whom they were framed and adopted, time and experience which tried all things, have demonstrated that they did not successfully meet the case. In a hurry and confusion of the hour and the eager desire to have the Union restored, there was more care for the sublime superstructure of the Republic, than for the solid foundation upon which alone it could be upheld.

They gave Freedmen the machinery of liberty but denied them the steam is to put it in motion. They gave them the uniform of soldiers, but no arms; they called them citizens, and left them subjects; they called them free and left them slaves.

They did not deprive the old master class of the power of life and death over their former slaves. Skin for skin as Satan said of Job: *that all a man hath will he give for his life.*

Now the man who has it in his power to say his fellow man, you must obey me or you shall starve, holds in his hands the power to make himself a master and his fellow man a slave, could the nation have been induced to listen to those stalwart Republicans, Thaddeus Stevens in Charles Sumner, some of the evils from which we now suffer would have been averted.

The Negro would not today be on his knees, as he is, supplicating the old master class to give him leave tutorial. He would not now be leaving the South as from a doomed city and seeking a

home in congenial climes but tilling the soil in comparative independence. He would not now be swindled out of his hard earnings
by money orders for wages with no money in them. He would not
be compelled to pay $10 per annum for an acre of ground, which
would not sell for more than half that some. He would not have to
pay four times more than a fair price for a pound of bacon as is now
the case, because left by our Emancipation measure at the mercy of
the men who have robbed him all his life and his people for centuries. Much complaint is made that the Freedmen have made so little
progress and have shown so little ability to take care of themselves
since their Emancipation. Is this just a complaint? Is it reasonable?
I neither think it just nor fair. To me, the wonder is not that the
freedmen have made so little progress; but that they have made so
much. Not that they have been standing still, but that they stand at
all. Reflect for a moment upon the situation in which these people
found themselves when they were liberated: consider their igno-
rance, poverty in destitution, and their absolute dependence upon
the class by which, for 200 years they have been held in bondage,
and you will be prepared to marvel that they have done so well as
they have. History does not furnish an example of Emancipation
under conditions less friendly to the emancipated class than was
ours. Liberty came to them, not in mercy, but in wrath; not by moral choice, but by military necessity; not by the people among whom
the freedmen were to live, and whose goodwill was essential to the
success of the measure; but by a people regarded as strangers and

foreigners, invaders and trespassers, aliens and enemies. The very manner of their emancipation naturally invited to the head of the freedmen the bitterest hostility. They were hated because they were free and hated because of those who had freed them. The old master class looked upon emancipation as one of the means by which rebellion had been overthrown in the South humiliated.

Nothing was to have been expected but that the old master class would endeavor as far as possible to make this great measure unsuccessful and odious. It was born in a tempest, in whirlwind and war, and he lived in a storm of violence in blood. When the Hebrews were emancipated, they were told to take spoil from the Egyptians. When the serfs of Russia were emancipated, they were given three acres of ground upon which they could live and make a living. But not so when our slaves were emancipated. They were sent away empty-handed, without money, without a foot of land to stand upon. Old and young in all conditions, sick and well, we're turned loose to the open sky, naked to their enemies. The old slave quarter that head before sheltered them in the fields that head yielded them corn, now denied them. The old master class, in their wrath, told them to clear out, the Yankees have freed you, now let them feed you and shelter you. Inhumane as this treatment it was the natural result of the bitter resentment felt by the old master class, And, in view of it, the wonder is not that the colored people of the South have done so little in the way of acquiring a comfortable living, but that they live at all. Taking all the circumstances into consideration, the colored people have no reason to despair. We still live, and while there is life, there is hope. The fact that we have endured wrongs and hardships, which would have destroyed any other race, and have increased in numbers in public consideration, I want to strengthen our faith in ourselves and our future. Let us then, wherever we are, whether at the North or the South, resolutely struggle on in the belief that there is a better day coming and that we by patience, industry, uprightness, and economy may hasten that better day. I will not listen to myself, and I would not have you listen to the nonsense that knows people can succeed in life among the people by whom they have been despised and oppressed. The statement is erroneous and contradicted by the whole history of human progress. A few centuries ago, all Europe was cursed with serfdom or slavery. Traces of this bondage may yet be discovered, but they are now so dim and shadowy is not to be seen with the naked eye. The Jews only a century ago were despised, hated and oppressed, but they have defied, met, and vanquished the hard conditions imposed upon them, and are now popular and powerful, and compel respect in all countries. Take courage from the example of all religious denominations that have sprung up since Martin Luther. Each, in its turn, has been oppressed and persecuted. Methodists, Baptists, and Quakers have all been compelled to feel the lash and sting of popular disfavor - yet all in their turn have conquered the prejudice and hate of their surroundings. Greatness does not come to any people on flowery beds of ease. We

As these two parties mainly divide the votes of the whole country, the alternative now before us is James A. Garfield the Republican, or Winfield Scott Hancock, the Democrat. Both parties are calling upon us in common with all other citizens for our voice, our work, and our vote for their respective candidates.

What answers shall we make, what answers should we make to these two political parties? Shall we say James A. Garfield Ohio, or Winfield Scott Hancock of Pennsylvania? Shall it be the National Republican Party or the sectional Democratic Party? Where shall we go? Before answering this question, allow me a word with respect to the nature of the canvas. To my mind, it is not so much a canvas of the merits of the parties. It is not so much who or what is Garfield or Hancock, but what is the character, composition tendencies, principles, aims, and ends of the respective parties by which they have been brought to the front and by which they are commended and supported. In other words, which of the two great parties shall dictate the policy and administer the national government during the four years succeeding the fourth of next March? Experience has demonstrated that this is not a government of persons, but of parties, that ours is not an autocracy, but a republic. There is in it a one-man power – but it is a power qualified by a written constitution, by political parties, and by the declared and settle judgment of the American people.

If at any time a president of the United States should take it into his head, that he is the State, that he is wise enough and strong enough to carry on this government without the support and cooperation of a party, or that he can make or unmake parties at his pleasure, he will find himself in deep water and in a sinking condition. All who have tried the experiment have miserably failed. John Tyler tried it and failed. Millard Fillmore tried it and failed Andrew Johnson tried it and failed. And no man will try it hereafter and succeed.

Parties are not made but grown. They do not originate with rulers, but with the people, enhance their power and vitality. In politics as well as elsewhere the whole, is more than a part, and many more than the few. Elihu Burnett used to say; it was better to be a small piece of something than a large piece of nothing. As the nation is more than a party, a party is more than an individual. The creator is even more than the creature. The candidate is not the creator of the party: but the party is the creator of the candidate. They have the power to lift up, and they have the power to cast down, and they have generally shown a pretty strong disposition to retain this power into exercise it when it required so to do. In a word, the party, whether it be the Democratic Party or the Republican Party, will be the power behind the Throne greater than the power of the Throne itself. Hence we should not exhaust the importance of the candidate above the party and enter into a contest about mere personal qualities or achievements; what should weigh and measure the parties which or to mold, guide, command, and control them.

But let there be no misconstruction here. Let no man imagine that in us subordinating the candidates to the great parties to which they belong that I either underestimate their importance or shrink from a comparison of their respective merits. I see nothing in the situation to suggest or impose this precedence. I hardly think that James A. Garfield has anything to fear from the most rigid and search in comparison with W. S. Hancock, equally certain, and I, that Chester A. Arthur cannot suffer by comparison with William H. English.

It is said in praise of General Hancock that when this country was in the throes of rebellion, and many of those who had been educated at West Point at the public expense were going over to the enemy, that he remains faithful and loyal; but so, did James A. Garfield. It is said that Hancock fought bravely, skillfully, and successfully to suppress the rebellion; so did James A. Garfield. Thus, in loyalty to the Union and in bravely fighting to maintain it against the slave-holding oligarchy that sought to overthrow it, Hancock gains nothing over Garfield in the comparison. Both men are entitled to the respect and gratitude of the American people for the part they took in that Supreme crisis. It is hard for men to be just, hard for an Englishman to be just to an Irishman, hard for an Irishman to be just to an Englishman, for a Christian to be just to a Jew, a white man to a Chinaman, or a Democrat to be just to a Republican – but I propose to be just to this loyal fighting Democrat at least. If either has the better of the other in the comparison thus far, the palm must be awarded to James a Garfield. Hancock was under special obligations of honor and duty to go into that war. He had been educated and trained at the public expense for that very contingency. That he did not meanly, traitorously, and cowardly skulk away or scamper away to the enemy as many of his democratic brethren did, is creditable alike to his head and heart. But neither the act nor the mold of a place is this me and one hair's breadth above Garfield. A West Point graduate, a military man by profession, in search of reputation at the cannon's mouth, must have felt it was a small sacrifice, and very strong temptation to take a hand in the war to suppress a rebellion.

On the other hand, there were special reasons why Garfield shouldn't hesitate and even decline the fiery ordeal. He was a man of peace by profession, taste in inclination. He was devoted to Art and Science, but not to the Art and Science of War. For him, the tented field had no attraction, and the blast of the bugle no music now: for such a man un-coerced by any special obligation. To drop all, at the first cry of danger and distress of his country, and bear his breast to the storm of war, should give him a higher place in our respect and esteem, then would be due to the educated, trained and necessarily ambitious warrior. When Garfield went to the war, it was not because he was, in legal phrase held in firmly bound to go - he but not as a bondman but as a free man. The motive and mainspring of his action were instinctive, spontaneous loyalty, and patriotism. I think well of military schools and standing armies.

with a view to deprive our people even of this imperfect protection and to make their subjection to the old master class full and complete.

Now to this utterance, more than to all his services to the Union cause, General Hancock is indebted for his nomination to the presidency of the United States by the Democratic Party. His services to the Union cause are to blind the North, and the order in which the sentiment appears is to win the South, but the main element that has brought him to the front, that he has since the war is the all-important question of protection to the Freedman, sympathized with the old master class. This is the statesmanship by which he is commended. One idea, one alone, and that is the subordination of loyal military power to rebel slave-holding civil power. Now, how stands the case of general Garfield? He has been in office and the public eye ever since the suppression of the rebellion. He has, during the last few years, since James G. Blaine left the House of Representatives, been the leader of that body, in the most conspicuous and commanding figure scene there. His name is a household word. His voice and vote have been given, and every important question has engaged the attention of the House of Representatives during the last 16 years. I need not refer to details to his record seen there; he has shown himself a clear-headed and thoughtful statement by his frequent and powerful vindication of the principles of justice and liberty in their body. I come back then, to the question, the all-important question, as to what an-

swer we are to make for these appeals for our voices and our votes.
In no relation, we sustain to our fellow man is wisdom more required than here. There is no calculating the good or the evil that
may come to our country and to ourselves from wise or foolish political action in association. Certainly, in order to vote wisely with
any party, we all have to have a clear understanding of its character,
composition, and tendencies. We should know what its principles
have been, its doctrines, and its measures. No man can be true to
himself, to his people, or to his country, who does not make himself master of this knowledge. Wherever else we may be stupid and
ignorant, here we are bound to be wide awake and intelligent. How
then shall this knowledge, so imperatively necessary to the public
good, be obtained? I answer, not by shutting our eyes and stopping
our ears, not by cultivating forgetfulness of the past and refusing to
look into the antecedents of a political party, not by blind trust in
the profession of individuals on the street or on the step who for
selfish purposes may conceal the truth from you.

There are men who would be miserable if they were wrong
due to the extent of a dime, who would without scruple mislead
you in politics. My advice to all, and especially to the colored people of this country, is that they search the heart and history of political parties that ask for their support. Let me first call attention
to the character, composition, principles, doctrines, and aims of the
Democratic Party and in dealing with that party. I find no place for
soft speech, delicate compliments, or patronizing disclaimers. Nei-

ther fear nor favor should come between the citizen and the stern duty of investigation. This is not the place for the elegant circum-locutions of the drawing-room and the parlor. Wherever else man be may be weak and effeminate, here they should be honest and still wart. We should be either hot or cold, one thing or the other. It offends my soul to hear a man talk as if one party were about as good as another as if he would keep an open door between them, so it is easy to glide from one to the other is interest or inclination may prompt. I am a Republican, a black Republican, a stalwart Republican, and I look at the Democratic Party from a Republican point of view and not from any middle ground between the two parties. I do not deny the possibility of reformation to any political party. It is composed of men, and men may be wiser and better in one generation than in another. Because a party pursued a bad and wicked end forty years ago – may not make it impossible, that it shall pursue a good one now. But we must take a rational view of probabilities and a stern view of facts as well; we should remember that the sins of the fathers descend to their children from generation to generation. From its very nature, the essential character of a political party is incapable of sudden and violent change, either from good to evil or from evil to good. It is, in fact, more likely to go from bad to worse than from good to better.

A stream flowing through a given channel wears where it is deeper, and deeper the longer it runs. To hear someone talk, you might think the character of a great party worn as a very loose garment – that it may be slipped on, and off without effort, and add a moment, or like a porous plaster to the back, easily removed or replaced with a little tepid water, or by holding it to a moderately warm smoothing iron. But the character of a political party is no loose garment and no plaster to the back. It is a part of the bone, muscle, fat, and fiber. It can be changed only by changing the air it breathes and the diet on which it lives. It may easily change its form, but not its substance. It may assume a virtue, even if it has not. Once at least in its life, the Democratic Party has giving given a striking example of the sort, of which I say more hereafter.

> *When the Devil was sick*
> *The Devil a Saint would be*
> *But when the Devil got well*
> *The Devil a Saint was he.*

Citation:

Douglass, Frederick. Speech Delivered at Elmira, N.Y. Manuscript/ Mixed Material. https://www.loc.gov/item/mfd.23019/.

From the Elmira *Daily Advertiser*, August 4, 1880 page 1

The Address of Hon. Frederick Douglass

The address, Hon. Frederick Douglass, delivered in the city yesterday, was an able and eloquent production, and every way worthy of the great reputation of the distinguished author. It abounds in invaluable information expressed eloquently in scholarly language and was full of suggestions for the guidance and improvement of his race. Although particularly intended for, and delivered to our colored citizens, it should be carefully read and thoroughly perused by every voter, no matter what may his nationality or the hue of his skin. It is a map of the situation drawn by one, as Mr. Douglass himself is expressive, who stands between the two races, and can't give advice to both. It is a calm, passionate and truthful history of the two great political parties of our country and shows beyond all doubt or question, which is the party of freedom in progress and the party of oppression and intolerance.

Postcard view of Hoffman's Grove (today's Grove Park). Circa 1900.
Published by Paul C. Koeber. Image collection of Diane Janowski.

From the Elmira *Daily Gazette* Aug 4 1880 page 5

The Colored People
How they Observed the Emancipation Anniversary
A Large Crowd and a Big Success

The events and successes of yesterday will long be remembered by the colored people of Elmira, and their numerous friends who came from other cities and villages to help them celebrate the anniversary of British liberation of slaves and the emancipation proclamation of Abraham Lincoln, merged in one grand day of enjoyment and commemoration.

Delegations were present from almost every considerable place within 100 miles of Elmira, and all the colored people were dressed in holiday attire, and there were the most smiling faces. The excitement reached the white folks, and long before noon, the hours set for the starting of the procession, the streets worth thronged with expecting people. The line was late in getting away from the rendezvous on Dickinson Street, but when it started, it was in the following order:

Grand marshal Hiram Washington, and assistant marshal Williams. Scott and Adams in command; the La France band, Mr. Daly, leader, and drum major, Benjamin. This band wore for the first time ever their new uniforms, dark blue, and the neatest we've ever seen on a band then came the Palmer Guards of Syracuse, a company of colored militia, 30 in line, of which William H. Franklin is Captain. They were accompanied by a large delegation of citizens from Geneva, led by B. F. Cleggett, and also accompanied by the Geddes Cornet Band, 15 in number; their leader is H. E. Tryon, and drum major, George Chapman; following these in the procession came the Elmira reception committee, followed by the Havana Cornet Band; their leader is E. C. Harding, 16 men with L. W. Swartwood, with a baton; a color barrier followed, then came the Horseheads Protection Company with 27 in line, Eugene Prince of Havana, Marshall of the Band, and Henry Scott of Geneva, assistant Marshall; Charles Brown is foreman, Andrew Dorsey, assistant foreman, and W. H. Dorsey also assistant foreman; the carriage containing John W. Jones, Esquire, President of the Day, Frederick Douglass, Orator, and William H. Lester, of Dryden, Reader, next came followed by the gentleman of the various committees and carriages; colored citizens of Corning were proceeded by the Corning Band, Walter Eggington, leader, and Cash J. Williams of Geneva, drum major; then came more flags, Reverend Mr. Collins and Reverend Mr. Smith, followed by citizens in carriages, in a long procession; the left of the line was brought by the gaily decorated wagon, drawn by four horses, containing 38 young ladies. The procession marched from Dickinson Street to Lake Street, down Lake to Water, Water to Main, Main to Church, Church to Walnut, and up Walnut to Hoffman's Grove.

John W. Jones of Elmira, New York, President of the Day.
Image collection of Diane Janowski.

The entire line was alive with spectators, and the most enthusiasm and interest were manifested on all sides. Many residents
were decorated in honor of our colored friends and visitors. There
was music all along the route; in fact, with so many bands, the air
was full of it, and no one could help being in sympathy with the
occasion. Having arrived at the Grove, which never was more in
splendid condition, the platform was possessed by the officers and
their speakers. The La France band went on stage and opened the
exercise with a fine selection of music. The Reverend Mr. Collins
offered prayer, and the President of the Day, Jones, formally opened
the meeting in a few happy and short remarks and introduced Mr.
W. H. Lester of Dryden, who read the emancipation proclamation
of Abraham Lincoln. Music by the band followed, with the Honorable Frederick Douglass, United States Marshal of the District
of Columbia, and the foremost colored man in the world was introduced. His appearance was loudly cheered, and this true lover
of his race delivered one of the strongest addresses ever heard in
Elmira. As the venerated and noble colored man stood on the platform, with his beard, his white and heavy locks, his massive frame
and kindly eyes, gave him the appearance of a Moses of his race. A
man who always singled out as a remarkable person, his presence
would be felt wherever he might be placed. His oration was long
and delivered from the manuscript; the speaker utters his sentences
deliberately, but his hearers never tire. He was frequently interrupt-
ed with applause at the utterance of some sentiment or laughter at

something thrust at the enemy. After the address, the meeting dispersed. Mr. Douglass left Elmira at 6:30 for Rochester.

Chief Knapp was present at Hoffman's Grove with three officers. No disturbances occurred, although there were present the usual white roughs, who were only deterred from making themselves obnoxious by the presence of restraint.

In the evening occurred the balls, and they were largely attended. The principal on was in the Military Hall under the auspices of the "Jolly Boys." It was a grand success and everything was conducted in first-class style. This was the largest attendance ever seen at Military Hall.

A ball occurred at the Academy of Music, under the auspices of the celebration officers. The music was by Pine's Full Orchestra. A sumptuous dinner was provided at the Wyckoff House on Water Street.

All in all, the day was a great success, and reflects great credit on the colored people, and especially on those of Elmira, who worked hard to make it a success.

More special edition reprinted books from

New York History Review

A Brief History of Chemung County, New York,
1779 -1905 with Index

Harper's New York & Erie Railroad Guide Book of 1851

The Elmira Prison Camp

Our Own Book : A Victorian Guide To Life

NewYorkHistoryReview.com

www.ingramcontent.com/pod-product-compliance
Lightning Source LLC
Chambersburg PA
CBHW022135280326
41933CB00007B/704